Faith to Conquer Fear

Inspiration to Achieve your Dreams

Christy L. Demetrakis

iUniverse, Inc.
New York   Bloomington

Faith to Conquer Fear
Inspiration to Achieve your Dreams

Copyright © 2010 by Christy L. Demetrakis

All rights reserved. No part of this book may be used or reproduced by any means, graphic, electronic, or mechanical, including photocopying, recording, taping or by any information storage retrieval system without the written permission of the publisher except in the case of brief quotations embodied in critical articles and reviews.

The views expressed in this work are solely those of the author and do not necessarily reflect the views of the publisher, and the publisher hereby disclaims any responsibility for them.

iUniverse books may be ordered through booksellers or by contacting:

iUniverse
1663 Liberty Drive
Bloomington, IN 47403
www.iuniverse.com
1-800-Authors (1-800-288-4677)

Because of the dynamic nature of the Internet, any Web addresses or links contained in this book may have changed since publication and may no longer be valid.

ISBN: 978-1-4502-6108-1 (sc)
ISBN: 978-1-4502-6109-8 (dj)
ISBN: 978-1-4502-6110-4 (ebk)

Library of Congress Control Number: 2010914130

Printed in the United States of America

iUniverse rev. date: 10/13/2010

This book is dedicated to those who harbor a God-given dream but need encouragement and inspiration to overcome fear and step out in faith.

Contents

Preface ix
Acknowledgments xi
Introduction xiii
Inspiration 1
Faith 7
Attitude 13
Confidence 19
Character 23
Determination 31
Dreams 37
Decisions 47
Change 53
Talent 63
Communication 69
Success 73
Epilogue 83
About the Author 85
Who's Quoted 87
Sources 99
The Empowered Speaker Company 101

Preface

Faith to Conquer Fear was birthed from a desire to encourage people to take steps toward achieving their dreams. As I have progressed through my professional and personal life over the last sixteen years, I have found the greatest inspiration for my achievements in the spoken word.

After graduating college, I harbored a dream of being a public speaker and coach. I knew this was not a passing fancy because for more than a decade, the desire never left my mind and my heart. I dreamed about it. I imagined myself on-stage. I thought about coaching others to be better public speakers. I knew that at some point I would have to reach this goal to feel personally fulfilled. However, for thirteen years, I always had excuses as to why the timing was not right:

- I need a source of income I can rely on.
- I need more credentials.
- I don't have enough time to build the business with my full-time job.
- I don't have the time to create a public speaking training program.

Finally, in 2007, I made the decision to bring this dream into reality. I created C & J Management, Inc., developed a web site, designed business cards, and invested in a certified instructor program for the Speakers Training Camp. The STC eliminated all of my excuses for not starting a business by setting the fees, providing certification, and allowing schedule flexibility and a packaged training program.

It took thirteen years and much encouragement from my friends, family, and pastors for me to build up the faith and confidence to start my business. Thirteen years is a long time to have a dream, but it went by in a moment. When I realized how quickly time passed, I knew I could not wait any longer. This is why I feel a passion, excitement, and urgency inside when I hear someone talk about dreams of owning a business, writing a book, or reaching a goal. I want you to stop thinking of all the reasons you cannot or should not try. *Faith to Conquer Fear* is about you stepping out in faith to accomplish what has been purposed in your heart. Let's get on with it!

Acknowledgments

To God, who is the head of my life, who knows the plans he has for me, who orders my steps and directs my paths.

To my husband, James, who consistently supports my career and my ambitions, no matter how far-fetched. You are the one constant when everything else changes.

To my parents, Eddie and Sherdina Sellars, who have always believed I can achieve anything I set my mind to. Mom, you are my best friend and a great encourager.

To my children, Mikayla and Collin, who do not always know what I am working on but support me nonetheless. I value your willingness to help brainstorm titles and ideas. A special thank-you goes to my daughter Mikayla, who acted as my "editor" and inspiration for examples and content within this book.

To my furry companion, Sophie, who is always willing to sacrifice her body to allow me to rub away the stresses of the day.

To pastors Dexter and Genette Howard, you have been instrumental in increasing my spiritual knowledge and understanding. Although I have spent my entire life in church, the growth I experienced in the three years under your teaching at Life Harvester Church was incredible. You created a servant mind-set that has influenced all of my actions ever since. I am a better person because of you.

To Bishop Michael Dantley and the wonderful people of Christ Emmanuel Christian Fellowship, for showing me there are new heights and dimensions in God.

To my friend Stephanie, who is a great sounding board for all of my grand ideas. You are a great supporter.

To my friend Cheryl, who is a great confidante. Thank you for praying for me without ceasing.

I love and appreciate you all!

Introduction

Do you remember sunny days, water hose sprinklers, ice cream trucks with their loud music playing, and mud pies? Remember when your only responsibility was to be in the house before dark? How about running around barefoot, throwing rocks over the utility lines, and riding bikes for hours on end and it didn't feel like exercise? That was the good life. Do you remember?

Now that you're all grown up, what do you associate with the good life and living well? Is it making lots of money and buying nice things? Is it traveling the world and experiencing different cultures? Is it being able to give back to those less fortunate? How do you define the good life?

When you reach adulthood, your perspective on life changes, your responsibilities change and increase, and your gauge of what's good absolutely changes. Financial independence and a sense of a higher purpose and peace are some elements of living the good life.

Let's talk financial independence. If you are like me, your ultimate goal when you go to work every day is to get paid, even though you may enjoy your job. Your priorities may be having a nice home, eating well, paying for college, traveling, and saving enough money to retire comfortably. You work to make money for yourself and your family. If the company makes money from your efforts in the process, then that's a mutual benefit. If you grew up in a poor to fairly middle-class environment, as an adult you most likely want financial independence and financial stability. If you grew up in a wealthy family, your objective may be to maintain or increase that standard of living. Financial independence allows you to enjoy life and live well.

Spiritual belief can lead to a gratifying life. Spirituality means different things to different people. If you believe in God the Father, Jesus the Son, and the Holy Spirit, spirituality represents a sense of connection to God. You have faith that sustains you even when circumstances around you are not ideal. You believe that when you pray earnestly, God will answer. You believe that you are blessed to be a blessing. God gives through you to give to others. You cannot go through this life only concerned about getting more and hoarding what you receive. The Bible says, in Luke 6:38, "Give and it will be given to you. A good measure, pressed down, shaken together, running over, will be poured into your lap. For with the measure you use, it will be measured to you." This means that the more you give, the more you receive. That is why the Bible says it is better to give than to receive. When you give, what you receive is multiplied. Blessing others can be gratifying.

When I was a child there was a gentleman in my parents' church who always said he prayed that his children would be good, law-abiding citizens. While that was a worthy prayer and his children turned out well, I have different expectations. I pray that my children will grow up with no harm coming to them. I pray that they are invisible to the enemy. I pray that they will one day marry their soul mates and have beautiful grandchildren for me and James to spoil. I pray that I will live to see them prosper and walk in their godly purpose. When all of that is accomplished, I will consider it a good life.

Last, but certainly not least, is peace. What is peace? Peace is that feeling you get when you've had a terrible day at work. You get home, open your door, and find your best furry friend waiting for you, healthy and happy, with his or her tail wagging. That's peace. Peace is what you feel when you've finally put the kids to bed and it's now "Mommy time." It is a time of serenity: a gentle breeze on a night when you can see all the stars, a warm bath, a good book while curled up on the couch, a chance to catch up on your favorite TV shows or flip through the pages of your favorite magazine.

What is peace to you? Is it peace in your home? Is it the knowledge that no matter how the world has treated you that day, when you go home, you have a spouse who loves you, beautiful children who are glad to see you, and a pet who adores you unconditionally?

How do you define the good life? Can you picture what it looks like for you? That life should not end with your childhood. It should remain with you as long as you are alive. Living your dream can get you to that place. Do not wait another day to take action toward the promise God has given you. Now is the time. We are given but one life. What do you choose to do with yours?

> There is only one success - to be able to spend your life in your own way.
> **Christopher Morley**

Inspiration

> Therefore encourage one another and build each
> other up, just as in fact you are doing.
> **1 Thessalonians 5:11 (NIV**

The 4th Edition American Heritage Dictionary defines inspiration as follows:

1. Stimulation of the mind or emotions to a high level of feeling or activity.
2. Something, such as a sudden creative act or idea, that is inspired.
3. Divine guidance or influence exerted directly on the mind and soul of humankind.

What inspires you? *Black Enterprise* magazine is a source of inspiration for me, especially when I read articles about everyday people turning seemingly small ideas into companies. Do you ever look at successful people and wonder what they did to become successful? Do you ever look at someone who is doing what you have envisioned for yourself and think, "I could do that, and perhaps better"? These questions should serve as inspiration and motivation for you. Are these people smarter than you? Probably not, but they have acted intelligently. Instead of sitting back and waiting to see if someone else is going to do it, they do it themselves. They see a need and fill it. They see an opportunity and seize it. These people find a way to accomplish while most sit back thinking of all the reasons why not. They forge ahead despite obstacles, desperate to succeed, and they never entertain the thought of failure.

How badly do you want it? Do you want to wake up one day and realize that time and opportunity have passed you by? My mom and I routinely talk during my commute to work. In 2004, I vividly remember a conversation we had about accomplishing things. I remember saying, "I do not want to wake up one day and realize that I have not accomplished any of the dreams I have. I do not want to leave this earth without having at least tried."

In my freshman year of college at the University of North Carolina in Chapel Hill, I declared a premed major. I actually thought for a full year that I was going to be a doctor. To this day I do not know what possessed me to think that was a viable option.

Universities and colleges are considered higher-level education institutions for a reason. The university does an excellent job of helping you to determine your strengths and weaknesses early in the process. At UNC, courses like Chemistry 11 are considered "weed-out" courses: the classes are large, instructors talk fast, and there are limited opportunities for students to ask clarifying questions. The sheer size and pace of the course discourages and weeds out those students who are either not willing or not able to pass and move on to Chemistry 21. I am pleased to say I had both the ability and the willingness to move on to Chemistry 21.

Unfortunately I encountered Biology 11 at about the same time. This was my weed-out course. In my entire educational career, I had never received a grade lower than a B. I received a D in that class and had to repeat the course in summer school. Can you say horrified?

My teary calls home to Mom grew more frequent until I took a speech class. One day after one of the speech classes, the teacher's assistant came to me and asked if I had considered majoring in speech communications. He recognized my talent for public speaking and shared all of the career options I could consider with a speech communications degree. His comments were the inspiration I needed to change my major and focus on what I had always enjoyed: public speaking. I graduated with a double major in speech communications and radio, television, and motion pictures. Sometimes life has to redirect your path.

If you knew that you had only one year to live, would that inspire you to pursue your goals or dreams? What would you try to accomplish in that year? Matthew Kelly, author of *The Dream Manager*, spoke at a Procter and Gamble training session I attended. As a part of the session, he conducted a "dream storming session," where each person wrote down answers to a series of questions as quickly as possible. He asked questions such as:

- What seven places have you always wanted to visit?
- If you could learn any foreign language, what would it be?
- If you could go back to school to study any topic, what would it be?

At the end of the session, he asked how many dreams had been written on the pads. The numbers ranged from thirty-two to better than a hundred. The revelation of the dream storming session was that dreams are often thought of as grandiose and unachievable. The concept of daydreaming has the connotation of dreaming of something that can never be achieved. In actuality, when you look at your own list of dreams, most of them can be implemented or executed as early as tomorrow with just a little planning.

You are given one life. William Penn said, "I expect to pass through life but once. If therefore, there be any kindness I can show, or any good thing I can do to any fellow being, let me do it now, and not defer or neglect it, as I shall not pass this way again." What do you choose to do with your life? You have to take control of your own destiny and act with the same sense of urgency that you would if you had only one year to accomplish your goals. What inspires you? Tap into that source of inspiration and move forward. Why wait to begin planning for your future reality?

> Reach high, for stars lie hidden in your soul. Dream deep, for every dream precedes the goal.
> **Ralph Vaull Starr**

> Failure will never overtake me if my determination to succeed is strong enough.
> **Og Mandino**

> We should be taught not to wait for inspiration to start a thing. Action always generates inspiration. Inspiration seldom generates action.
> **Frank Tibolt**

> So long as there is breath in me, that long will I persist. For now I know one of the greatest principles of success; if I persist long enough I will win.
> **Og Mandino**

> It isn't where you come from; it's where you're going that counts.
> **Ella Fitzgerald**

Quotes are nothing but inspiration for the uninspired.
Richard Kemph

What this country needs is more people to inspire others with confidence, and fewer people to discourage any initiative in the right direction, more to get into the thick of things, fewer to sit on the sidelines merely finding fault, more to point out what's right with the world, and fewer to keep harping on what's wrong with it and more who are interested in lighting candles, and fewer who blow them out.
Father James Keller

Prepare your mind to receive the best that life has to offer.
Ernest Holmes

Faith

He replied, "Because you have so little faith. I tell you the truth, if you have faith as small as a mustard seed, you can say to this mountain, 'Move from here to there' and it will move. Nothing will be impossible for you."
Matthew 17:20

Pastor Genette Howard of Life Harvester Church International in Fayetteville, Arkansas, once made a great analogy between children and arrows. The distance an arrow travels is based on how far you pull the arrow back on the bow. The farther you pull the arrow back, the farther it goes forward. Children are like arrows.

As parents we aim our children in the direction they should go. Sometimes parents have to pull their children back from some things early in life so they can soar later. God propels His children forward toward destiny in the same way. But in order for you to reach the destiny and position God has designed, you must have faith in the direction he has aimed you.

As children, the direction we received often came from parents or grandparents, and we had faith and confidence that our parents knew what was best. Parents have a vested interest in their children. God commands parents to train up a child in the way he should go. That is the basis for the confidence that you could trust your parents and their instruction. God desires for you to have an even greater level of confidence and faith in Him.

Faith expresses your confidence in God. It says that you take God at His word, the same way you took your parents at their word as a young child. Faith is the vehicle that takes you to God's promise for your life.

The fact that faith is a process often trips people up. It is a journey. Faith comes on the heels of trials and setbacks. It is developed over time. Faith is not for obtaining what you want. It is for believing God. Faith is what will help you to believe in the feasibility of your dream. Other people do not have to believe in what you want to achieve. Only you have to believe it. You have to believe it for as long as it takes to achieve the promise. If God has promised you a business, then have faith and believe until that new business comes into existence. Too many times your blessing stalls because of impatience. Just because you have not seen the promise yet does not mean it is not coming. Time is not working against you; it is working for you.

There is a season for everything under the sun. There is always a period of time between "I believe" and "I receive." When you plant a tomato seed, you don't refer to it as a tomato seed. You say "I'm planting a tomato." You already see it as a tomato even though it is just a seed. You believe in the promise of the tomato developing from the seed. When you plant the tomato seed, you have no control over making the seed grow. All of the work is done inside of the seed. Your job is to nurture the seed and ensure the atmosphere is right for its growth into a fully edible tomato. Faith and belief is the way you nurture the promise God has given you so that it may come to fruition, just like the tomato.

> Faith is deliberate confidence in the character of God whose ways you may not understand at the time.
> **Oswald Chambers**

> Faith is taking the first step even when you don't see the whole staircase.
> **Martin Luther King Jr.**

The first step is to fill your life with a positive faith that will help you through anything. The second is to begin where you are.
Norman Vincent Peale

I tell you the truth, anyone who has faith in me will do what I have been doing. He will do even greater things than these, because I am going to the Father. And I will do whatever you ask in my name, so that the Son may bring glory to the Father.
John 14:12–13

> Faith is the belief "it is" before it is and the comfort of it coming before it arrives.
> **Unknown Author**

I tell you the truth, if anyone says to this mountain, "Go, throw yourself into the sea," and does not doubt in his heart but believes that what he says will happen, it will be done to him.
Mark 11:23

Faith is not belief without proof, but trust without reservation.
Unknown Author

Whatever you ask for in prayer, believe that you
have received it, and it will be yours.
Mark 11:24

It is impossible to be a hero in anything
unless one is first a hero in faith.
Jacobi

When you have come to the edge Of all light that you know
And are about to drop off into the darkness Of the unknown,
Faith is knowing One of two things will happen: There will
be something solid to stand on or You will be taught to fly.
Patrick Overton

Faith isn't faith until it's all you're holding on to.
Unknown Author

To one who has faith, no explanation is necessary.
To one without faith, no explanation is possible.
St. Thomas Aquinas

Ask and it will be given to you; seek and you will
find; knock and the door will be opened to you.
Matthew 7:7

Faith is to believe what you do not see; the reward
of this faith is to see what you believe.
St. Augustine

I tell you that if two of you on earth agree about
anything you ask for, it will be done for you by
my Father in heaven. For where two or three come
together in my name, there am I with them.
Matthew 18:19-20

We get new ideas from God every hour of our day when we put our trust in Him -- but we have to follow that inspiration up with perspiration -- we have to work to prove our faith. Remember that the bee that hangs around the hive never gets any honey.
Albert E. Cliffe

The only thing that stands between a man and what he wants from life is often merely the will to try it and the faith to believe that it is possible.
David Viscott

Attitude

> Do not conform any longer to the pattern of this world, but be transformed by the renewing of your mind. Then you will be able to test and approve what God's will is—his good, pleasing and perfect will.
> **Romans 12:2**

"What if I fail?" How are you going to fail if you never start? Michael Jordan once stated, "I can accept failure, but I can't accept not trying." One thing is certain. You absolutely will not fail if you do not try. If you meet a person who has never failed, you are in the presence of a person who has never tried.

Some people are not even willing to articulate their dreams for fear of what people will say. "What would my family think if they knew that I wanted to…?" The familiar saying "Attitude determines your altitude" is so true. If you embrace a defeatist attitude, the results of your endeavors will be defeat. Those with positive attitudes expect positive results. For those people, if the outcome is not positive, they believe it will be the next time. A positive attitude is what drives them to keep trying.

Imagine a child on the playground standing all alone watching the other kids play kickball. When asked why he isn't playing, he says, "I don't think I'd be very good at it, so I don't even want to try." How would you respond? Would you say, "Its okay. You can just stand here and watch." Or would you say, "Have you ever tried kickball? I bet if you made an effort, the other kids would let you play. You might even like it! Give it a try." Sometimes you need to think more like a child. Most children do not recognize their limitations until an adult tells them they cannot do something. They have a can-do attitude.

A few years ago, my eight-year-old son began playing football. By Kentucky standards he was learning football late in life. That first year was an extremely steep and painful learning curve, but he had inherited his father's athletic prowess. His team practiced three to four times per week, and at least twice a week I ran Epsom salt baths to soothe his aching body. On many occasions he cried and complained that the coach's expectations of him were too high. "I just started playing this year, and they expect me to know all the plays." Like any good mother, I listened sympathetically and offered encouragement that things would get better. However, midway through the season, I had heard enough of the whining. It was time for tough love.

"Do you want to play football?" I said.

He responded, "Yes, but—"

"There are no 'buts'. If you are tired of being yelled at for not knowing the plays, then learn the plays. You are a smart kid. If you do not know the plays by now, then it's your own fault. Your father is an all-American football player who would love nothing more than to teach you everything he knows. You have an advantage that you are not leveraging. Learn the plays, learn the game, and stop complaining." His attitude slowly changed, and his performance improved. In Collin's second year of football, he was named linebacker of the year for the league and was an all-star for his team.

Think about your circle of friends. Do you prefer positive, confident people or people who are always negative and have nothing good to say? In general, people prefer to be around those who are positive and forward thinking. The litmus test is the elevator. If you were stuck in an elevator, would you want to be stuck with another you? If not, change your attitude.

> Attitude is more important than the past, than education, than money, than circumstances, than what people do or say. It is more important than appearance, giftedness, or skill.
> **Charles Swindoll**

> You must accept that you might fail; then, if you do your best and still don't win, at least you can be satisfied that you've tried. If you don't accept failure as a possibility, you don't set high goals, you don't branch out, you don't try – you don't take the risk.
> **Rosalynn Carter**

> I have not failed. I've just found 10,000 ways that won't work.
> **Thomas Edison**

> Pain is temporary. Quitting lasts forever.
> **Lance Armstrong**

> When one door closes, another opens; but we often look so long and so regretfully upon the closed door that we do not see the one which has opened for us.
> **Alexander Graham Bell**

> Begin with the end in mind.
> **Stephen Covey**

Achievement seems to be connected with action. Successful men and women keep moving. They make mistakes, but they don't quit.
Conrad Hilton

For success, attitude is equally as important as ability.
Harry F. Banks

Things may not always be packaged the way you want them, but if it's a gift, you take it.
Christy Demetrakis

Ability is what you're capable of doing. Motivation determines what you do. Attitude determines how well you do it.
Lou Holtz

Up to a point a man's life is shaped by environment, heredity, and movements and changes in the world about him; then there comes a time when it lies within his grasp to shape the clay of his life into the sort of thing he wishes to be. Everyone has it within his power to say, this I am today, that I shall be tomorrow.
Louis L'Amour

Sometimes we are limited more by attitude than by opportunities.
Anonymous

The only place where dreams are impossible is in your own mind.
Emalie

There are two big forces at work, external and internal. We have very little control over external forces such as tornadoes, earthquakes, floods, disasters, illness and pain. What really matters is the internal force. How do I respond to those disasters? Over that I have complete control.
Leo Buscalgia

Whether you believe you can do a thing or not, you are right.
Henry Ford

Confidence

So do not throw away your confidence;
it will be richly rewarded.
Hebrews 10:35

"I think I can. I think I can. I think I can." We have all heard this mantra, first introduced by author Watty Piper in his book *The Little Engine That Could*. This is a story of an engine that is stranded on train tracks and needs to be pulled over a large hill. Several other larger and more impressive trains refuse to help the broken-down train. Along comes Tillie, a little blue engine who is willing to help the stranded train despite its small size. Ignoring criticism and skepticism from the other trains, Tillie pulls the larger train over a huge hill while chanting, "I think I can. I think I can. I think I can."

This is a story of risk, belief, and confidence. Even though Tillie was small, the little blue engine was willing to try, which means it was also willing to fail. Are you afraid to succeed, or are you afraid to fail? In analyzing Tillie's story, one could argue that the larger engines refused to help the stranded engine because they were not certain they could actually get the stranded engine over the large hill. You cannot fail if you do not try, right? Tillie was willing to take the risk even though the odds of success were slim.

Secondly, Tillie knew that sometimes you have to encourage and believe in yourself even when others do not. This is an excellent example of mind over matter. Tillie's mantra, "I think I can. I think I can. I think I can," was the motivation needed to keep those little wheels turning and to pull the larger engine up and over the hill. The hill in this story is symbolic for the challenges you face that sometimes drain your confidence.

Lastly, Tillie possessed confidence. It all started with a thought. "I think I can" Tillie spoke belief until it came to pass. "I think I can. I think I can. I think I can." That is how it starts, with an inner belief in what you can achieve. The important thing to note is Tillie did not speak the belief before starting the journey. On the contrary, the little blue engine encouraged itself while pulling the larger engine over the hill. And even while pulling, the little engine was not entirely certain it could accomplish the task, but Tillie kept moving forward in the effort.

Confidence comes from within. People can have confidence in you and your abilities. However, if you do not have confidence in yourself, your efforts will be in vain. You do not always have to wait to be fully confident in the outcome. Encourage and believe in yourself while moving forward.

> One important key to success is self-confidence. An important key to self-confidence is preparation.
> **Arthur Ashe**

> Confidence is the companion of success.
> **Anonymous**

Learn from the mistakes of others. You can't live
long enough to make them all yourself.
Eleanor Roosevelt

In each of us are places where we have never gone.
Only by pressing the limits do you ever find them.
Dr. Joyce Brothers

Clothes and manners do not make the man; but when
he is made, they greatly improve his appearance.
Arthur Ashe

God, grant me the serenity
To accept things that I cannot change;
The courage to change the things I can;
And the wisdom to know the difference.
Dr. Reinhold Niebuhr

Regardless of how you feel inside, always try to look like a winner. Even if you are behind, a sustained look of control and confidence can give you a mental edge that results in victory.
Arthur Ashe

Confidence is the hinge on the door to success.
Mary O'Hare Dumas

You gain strength, courage, and confidence by every experience in which you really stop to look fear in the face. You must do the thing which you think you cannot do.
Eleanor Roosevelt

Do not let what you cannot do interfere with what you can do.
John Wooden

Character

Do not be misled: "Bad company corrupts good character."
1 Corinthians 15:33

One's character is best revealed in times of success or adversity. Maya Angelou once said, "The first time someone shows you who they are, believe them." The Bible provides real-life examples of character. In the Bible, the stories of Job, Noah, and King Herod showcase character in the midst of great adversity.

Job was a wealthy man. According to the Bible, he had seven sons, three daughters, seven thousand sheep, three thousand camels, five hundred teams of oxen, five hundred donkeys, and a large staff of servants. He was a man of means. Even though Job had considerable wealth, he was a man of reputable character. God considered him to be faithful, upright, and moral. Because Job had shown himself to be a true follower of God, he allowed Satan to test Job's allegiance to him through a series of trials and tribulations. Satan believed he could prove that Job was faithful to God only because he had provided great wealth to Job. God believed in Job's character and allowed Satan to test his theory.

Job endured two tests from Satan. During the first test, Satan destroyed his family and finances. Job's oxen, donkeys, and camels were stolen. His sheep were struck by lightning and killed. His children were killed by a tornado when the house collapsed on them. All Job's earthly wealth was gone, yet he still worshipped God and did not sin. Satan was not satisfied with this response, so he asked God to let him test an affliction against Job's health. Satan inflicted painful sores over Job's body, from the top of his head to the soles of his feet. Though Job could not rest or find any relief, he did not sin. In God's eyes, Job's character remained intact.

Noah was considered a righteous man in the Bible. He was the builder of the famous ark. God commanded Noah to create the ark to hold both Noah's family and two of every species for procreation after God brought the great flood that killed every other living being on earth. God chose to save Noah and his family because Noah had shown honorable character over the years. He was obedient to God and was rewarded for that obedience and righteousness.

King Herod was the king of Judea in 37 bc. Some historians would say that Herod had a successful reign as king. However, he was a ruthless king who did whatever acts necessary to achieve his goals. During his tenure King Herod ordered the killing of all male infants in Bethlehem two years of age and under in order to eliminate potential successors. He is known for imprisoning and beheading John the Baptist at the request of his wife, who was previously his brother's wife. King Herod knew John the Baptist was a righteous and holy man, yet he beheaded him to save face among the guests at his dinner party.

Job, Noah, and King Herod handled adversity in different ways. Job praised God despite his losses and suffering. Noah remained obedient to God, carefully following His instructions.

Noah did not take advantage of the fact he had favor with God. He was diligent. King Herod, on the contrary, was greedy and prideful. When adverse situations arose, he did whatever was necessary to ensure that his position as king remained intact.

Character affects the outcome of your journey. If you use Noah, Job, and King Herod as examples of an expected end, Noah died a peaceful death in his sleep. Job was restored from his physical ailments after he prayed for his friends. King Herod, on the other hand, suffered greatly in death. He died an excruciating death from a combination of gangrene, chronic kidney disease, and scabies. Now clearly all of those with good character do not have a life free of suffering. Nor do all those with poor character come to a horrible demise. However, the Bible is true in Galatians 6:7-8: "Do not be deceived: God cannot be mocked. A man reaps what he sows. The one who sows to please his sinful nature, from that nature will reap destruction; the one who sows to please the Spirit, from the Spirit will reap eternal life."

> With integrity you have nothing to fear, since you have nothing to hide. With integrity you will do the right thing, so you will have no guilt. With fear and guilt removed you are free to be and do your best.
> **Zig Ziglar**

> I admire men of character and I judge character not by how men deal with their superiors, but mostly how they deal with their subordinates. And that, to me, is where you find out what the character of a man is.
> **General H. Norman Schwarzkopf**

> Success is always temporary. When all is said and done, the only thing you'll have left is your character.
> **Vince Gill**

Success builds character, failure reveals it.
Dave Checketts

The higher up you go, the more gentle you have to reach down to help other people succeed.
Rick Castro

Ability can take you to the top, but it takes character to keep you there.
Zig Ziglar

Champions do not become champions when they win the event, but in the hours, weeks, months, and years they spend preparing for it. The victorious performance itself is merely the demonstration of their championship character.
T. Alan Armstrong

Love never fails; character never quits; and with patience and persistence; dreams do come true.
Pete Maravich

When you choose your friends, don't be short-changed by choosing personality over character.
W. Somerset Maugham

If you call yourself leading and nobody's following, you're just taking a walk.
Bishop Michael Dantley

1. Marry the right person. This one decision will determine 90% of your happiness or misery.
2. Work at something you enjoy and that's worthy of your time and talent.
3. Give people more than they expect and do it cheerfully.

4. Become the most positive and enthusiastic person you know.
5. Be forgiving of yourself and others.
6. Be generous.
7. Have a grateful heart.
8. Persistence, persistence, persistence.
9. Discipline yourself to save money on even the most modest salary.
10. Treat everyone you meet like you want to be treated.
11. Commit yourself to constant improvement.
12. Commit yourself to quality.
13. Understand that happiness is not based on possessions, power or prestige, but on relationship with people you love and respect.
14. Be loyal.
15. Be honest.
16. Be a self-starter.
17. Be decisive even if it means you'll sometimes be wrong.
18. Stop blaming others. Take responsibility for every area of your life.
19. Be bold and courageous. When you look back on your life, you'll regret the things you didn't do more than the ones you did.
20. Take good care of those you love.
21. Don't do anything that wouldn't make your Mom proud.

H. Jackson Brown Jr.

A "No" uttered from deepest conviction is
better and greater than a "Yes" merely uttered to
please, or what is worse, to avoid trouble.
Mohandas Karamchand Gandhi

The true test of character is not how much we know how to do, but how we behave when we don't know what to do.
Jon Holt

You can tell the character of every man when you see how he receives praise.
Lucius Annæus Seneca

Show me a man who cannot bother to do little things and I'll show you a man who cannot be trusted to do big things.
Lawrence Bell

What we think or what we believe is, in the end, of little consequence. The only thing of consequence is what we do.
John Ruskin

The discipline you learn and character you build from setting and achieving a goal can be more valuable than the achievement of the goal itself.
Bo Bennett

Our character is what we do when we think no one is looking.
Jackson Browne

The circumstances amid which you live determine your reputation; the truth you believe determines your character.
Reputation is what you are supposed to be; character is what you are.
Reputation is the photograph; character is the face.
Reputation comes over one from without; character grows up from within.
Reputation is what you have when you come to a new community; character is what you have when you go away.
Your reputation is learned in an hour; your character does not come to light for a year.

Reputation is made in a moment; character is built in a lifetime.
Reputation grows like a mushroom;
character grows like the oak.
A single newspaper report gives you your reputation;
a life of toil gives you your character.
Reputation makes you rich or makes you poor;
character makes you happy or makes you miserable.
Reputation is what men say about you on your tombstone;
character is what angels say about you before the throne of God.
William Hersey Davis

Surely what a man does when he is taken off his guard is the best evidence for what sort of a man he is. Surely what pops out before the man has time to put on a disguise is the truth. If there are rats in a cellar you are most likely to see them if you go in very suddenly. But the suddenness does not create the rats: it only prevents them from hiding. In the same way the suddenness of the provocation does not make me an ill-tempered man; it only shows me what an ill-tempered man I am. The rats are always there in the cellar, but if you go in shouting and noisily they will have taken cover before you switch on the light.
Clive Staples Lewis

It's good to have money and the things that money can buy, but it's good, too, to make sure you haven't lost the things that money can't buy.
George Horace Lorimer

Thank God every morning you get up and find you have something to do that must be done, whether you like it or not. That builds character.
James Russell Lowell

Be more concerned with your character than your reputation, because your character is what you really are, while your reputation is merely what others think you are.
John Wooden

An old Cherokee is teaching his grandson about life: "A fight is going on inside me," he said to the boy. "It is a terrible fight and it is between two wolves. One is evil - he is anger, envy, sorrow, regret, greed, arrogance, self-pity, guilt, resentment, inferiority, lies, false pride, superiority, and ego. The other is good - he is joy, peace, love, hope, serenity, humility, kindness, benevolence, empathy, generosity, truth, compassion, and faith. This same fight is going on inside you - and inside every other person, too."
The grandson thought about it for a minute and then asked his grandfather, "Which wolf will win?"
The old Cherokee simply replied, "The one you feed."
American Indian Proverb

Determination

> In his heart a man plans his course, but
> the LORD determines his steps.
> **Proverbs 16:9**

You can learn about determination by watching your pets. Our dog Sophie is a four-year-old shimo. She is a "designer hybrid" mixture of American Eskimo and shih tzu. Whatever her combination, she is the most loved being in the house. Everybody loves Sophie. Her sweet personality and willingness to sacrifice her body to be rubbed for hours on end has converted many visitors who were afraid of dogs into dog lovers.

Sophie is a very smart girl. Every night before bedtime, she goes out to do the "pee pee mambo". She is well aware that after this great accomplishment she receives a cookie from the cookie jar. She runs back to the door, herds me to the kitchen, and stands on her hind legs in anticipation of the cookie reward.

Although Sophie is highly intelligent and understands the process required for getting a cookie, she likes to test the rules every now and then. Her routine usually begins with her coming over to be rubbed, which we have no problem doing on demand. After I'm finished rubbing her, she goes over to my husband, who repeats the process. She repeats the process with a greater sense of urgency, which immediately leads me to believe the kids forgot to feed her dinner. I ask, "Did anyone feed Sophie?" That's her cue. She's got me now. She begins running in circles, following me around the kitchen and walking on her hind legs, all the while getting closer to the cookie jar. At this point, one of two things happens. In the first scenario, my son runs down the stairs to feed Sophie because he forgot. Sophie is appeased because she really is hungry. In the second scenario, I look at Sophie's bowl and realize she has chosen not to eat her food and is really hoping she can skip right to dessert. Now what would you do? She has snuggled, run around in circles, and walked on her hind legs. She has shown great determination. Sophie gets a treat. Sophie's determination and persistence helped her to achieve her goal. This same single-minded focus works for humans as well. Once you have purposed something in your heart, the opportunities begin to manifest themselves.

Abraham Lincoln was a great example of determination. Most only hear the story of Abraham Lincoln, the president who signed the Emancipation Proclamation and freed the slaves. However, the sixteenth president of the United States suffered many setbacks in his quest for the most coveted political office in the country.

Lincoln encountered numerous obstacles in business, life, and politics between the years of 1831 and 1865. After his father relocated the family to Illinois, Lincoln struck out on his own to New Salem. He was hired by a general store owner to take boatload cargo from New Salem to New Orleans. Not long after Lincoln was offered the cashier position at the store, the business failed, forcing him to find other work.

Faith to Conquer Fear

In 1832, at the age of twenty-three, Abe Lincoln began his foray into politics. He announced his candidacy for the Illinois General Assembly. He did not have money, a formal education, or powerful friends. When the election was over, he finished eighth out of thirteen candidates. It was not a great first showing. However, two years later, Lincoln won the election to the Illinois state legislature.

Abraham Lincoln suffered several heartbreaks in his personal life over the years. His first love and fiancé died of typhoid fever in 1835. As a result, he had a nervous breakdown and was bedridden for six months. He later married and had four sons. He and his wife Mary's second child died of tuberculosis at age four. A second son died of a fever at age eleven.

Lincoln's political career continued to have peaks and valleys. In 1843, he ran for Congress and lost. He ran again in 1846 and won but lost reelection in 1848. In 1854 and 1856, Lincoln ran for the Senate and the vice-presidential nomination. He lost again. In fact, he only received one hundred votes for the vice president nomination. Abraham Lincoln ran for Senate again in 1858 and lost.

Despite having enough defeats and obstacles during his career to deter most anyone, Abraham Lincoln persevered. He had determination. He kept trying until he achieved the highest political office in the United States. He won the presidency in 1860.

Some men succeed because they are destined to, but most men succeed because they are determined to.
Graeme Clegg

The person interested in success has to learn to view failure as a healthy, inevitable part of the process of getting to the top.
Dr. Joyce Brothers

Patience, persistence, and perspiration make
an unbeatable combination for success.
Napoleon Hill

Obstacles don't have to stop you. If you run into a
wall, don't turn around and give up. Figure out how
to climb it, go through it, or work around it.
Michael Jordan

Courage doesn't always roar. Sometimes courage is the quiet
voice at the end of the day saying, "I will try again tomorrow."
Mary Anne Radmacher

You can do what you have to do, and sometimes you
can do it even better than you think you can.
Jimmy Carter

Nothing in the world can take the place of persistence.
Talent will not; nothing is more common than unsuccessful
men with talent. Genius will not; unrewarded genius is
almost a proverb. Education alone will not; the world is
full of educated derelicts. Persistence and determination
alone are omnipotent. The slogan "press on" has solved
and always will solve the problems of the human race.
John Calvin Coolidge

No one ever attains very eminent success by simply
doing what is required of him; it is the amount and
excellence of what is over and above the required that
determines the greatness of ultimate distinction.
Charles Kendall Adams

What am I willing to sacrifice for what I want to become?
Anonymous

I'd rather be a could-be if I cannot be an are; because a could-be is a maybe who is reaching for a star. I'd rather be a has-been than a might-have-been, by far; for a might have-been has never been, but a has was once an are.
Milton Berle

Life's real failure is when you do not realize how close you were to success when you gave up.
Unknown Author

Perseverance is more than endurance. It is endurance combined with absolute assurance and certainty that what we are looking for is going to happen.
Oswald Chambers

When things go wrong as they sometimes will, When the road you're trudging seems all up hill, When the funds are low and the debts are high, And you want to smile, but you have to sigh, When care is pressing you down a bit, Rest if you must, but don't you quit. Life is queer with its twists and turns, As every one of us sometimes learns, And many a failure turns about, When he might have won had he stuck it out. Don't give up though the pace seems slow--You may succeed with another blow, Success is failure turned inside out--The silver tint of the clouds of doubt, And you never can tell how close you are, It may be near when it seems so far; So stick to the fight when you're hardest hit--It's when things seem worst that you must not quit.
Unknown Author

Dreams

> In the last days, God says,
> I will pour out my Spirit on all people.
> Your sons and daughters will prophesy,
> your young men will see visions,
> your old men will dream dreams.
> **Acts 2:17**

Have you ever had a dream that you've held close for years, for as long as you can remember? What keeps you from acting on that dream?

- Age?
- Time commitments?
- Children?
- Capital investment too high?
- Afraid to quit your current job?

Perhaps you just do not know how to start. How can you make money? Do you really *want* to do this? What if you are not as good as you think you are? All the time you are thinking, the clock is ticking. As long as you are second-guessing your abilities and the potential cost of your dream, you are not moving forward. You are not making any progress. You have effectively paralyzed yourself with all of these questions.

Golden opportunities are seasonal, just like the cresting of a river. The Jordan River in southwest Asia flows through the Great Rift Valley into the Dead Sea. The Jordan is shallow. However, it has seasons of high water and low water. Its high water period lasts from January to March, while its low water period occurs at the end of summer and the beginning of autumn. This river has great significance in the Bible. Jesus was baptized by John the Baptist in the Jordan. Healing took place in its waters. The Jordan was also a source of water for the lands along its edges. When the water levels were low, people could walk across the Jordan. It was more difficult to cross when the water was at its highest point. In biblical times, the people recognized when the time was right: at the end of the summer and the beginning of autumn. The window of opportunity does not remain open indefinitely just as the Jordan River does not remain shallow indefinitely. If you miss your window, you will have to wait that much longer to reach your destination.

Your dream may be to create a witty invention. It could be completing your list of goals to achieve over your lifetime, earning your high school diploma, or college degree. You may have a desire to completely change careers. Whatever the dream, it's time to wake up and get out of bed! One of my favorite movies of all time is *Sister Act 2: Back in the Habit*. There is a scene in the movie where the choir sings a song.

> If you wanna be somebody,
> If you wanna go somewhere,
> You better wake up and pay attention.

Defining whether your dream is something you *want* to do or *need* to do will determine how hard you are willing to work to achieve it. If you simply *want* to achieve, the outcome may look more like a hobby than a potential career. There are no defined goals and timelines developed to ensure you are on track. There is no fear of either success or failure. On the other hand, if you feel the *need* to reach the goal because it is your God-given calling, your actions look significantly different. There is urgency in your actions. You constantly seek information and ways to implement and improve the plan. The goal is always in the back of your mind. You wake up and go to bed thinking about what you need to do to move forward.

In the movie *Sister Act 2: Back in the Habit*, the character named Rita, played by Lauren Hill, is a teenager at a Catholic school who has a beautiful singing voice. The nuns in the school decide to form a choir made up of students in the music class. Rita is passionate about singing. It's what she loves, and she dreams of being a singer. However, her mother does not support her dream because her father had tried to become a professional singer and never succeeded. The mother had a very negative perception about singing for a living, and her attitude disheartened Rita. At one point in the movie, Rita dropped out of the school's choir. One day, one of the nuns overheard Rita singing at the piano in the school. The nun asked Sister Mary Clarence, played by Whoopi Goldberg, to talk her into coming back to the choir. While the movie is a comedy, Sister Mary Clarence's words to Rita were very insightful. She told Rita that as a child she wanted to be a singer. She went to her mother, who gave her a book by Rainer Maria Rilke entitled *Letters to a Young Poet*. "A fellow used to write to him and say, 'I wanna be a writer, please read my stuff.' And Rilke says to this guy, 'Don't ask me about being a writer. If when you wake up in the morning you can think of nothing but writing, then you're a writer.' I'm gonna say the same thing to you. If you wake up every morning and you can't think of anything but singing first, then you're supposed to be a singer, girl."

Christy L. Demetrakis

Your mind does not have the ability to think or imagine something that cannot be created. If you can dream it, the dream can become reality, even if you do not create it yourself. The dream was put in your spirit for a reason. It was not given to anyone else in the same measure that was given to you. No one else can see the intricate details of your dream as you can. Langston Hughes wrote a poem entitled "A Dream Deferred":

> What happens to a dream deferred?
> Does it dry up
> like a raisin in the sun?
> Or fester like a sore--
> And then run?
> Does it stink like rotten meat?
> Or crust and sugar over--
> like a syrupy sweet?
> Maybe it just sags
> like a heavy load.
> Or does it explode?

Every great dream begins with a dreamer. Always remember, you have within you the strength, the patience, and the passion to reach for the stars to change the world.
Harriet Tubman

The man who has no imagination has no wings.
Muhammad Ali

In life, many thoughts are born in the course of a moment, an hour, a day. Some are dreams, some visions. Often, we are unable to distinguish between them. To some, they are the same; however, not all dreams are visions. Much energy is lost in fanciful dreams that never bear fruit. But visions are messages from the Great Spirit, each for a different purpose in life. Consequently, one person's vision may not be that of another. To have a vision, one must be prepared to receive it, and when it comes, to accept it. Thus when these inner urges become reality, only then can visions be fulfilled. The spiritual side of life knows everyone's heart and who to trust. How could a vision ever be given to someone to harbor if that person could not be trusted to carry it out. The message is simple: commitment precedes vision.
High Eagle

Nothing happens unless first a dream.
Carl Sandburg

Without leaps of imagination, or dreaming, we lose the excitement of possibilities. Dreaming, after all, is a form of planning.
Gloria Steinem

To accomplish great things, we must not only act, but also dream; not only plan, but also believe.
Anatole France

The best way to make your dreams come true is to wake up.
Paul Valery

Only as high as I reach can I grow, only as far as I seek can I go, only as deep as I look can I see, only as much as I dream can I be.
Karen Ravn

What other people label or might try to call failure, I have learned is just God's way of pointing you in a new direction.
Oprah Winfrey

If you're not failing every now and again, it's a sign you're not doing anything very innovative.
Woody Allen

The gem cannot be polished without friction, nor man perfected without trials.
Chinese Proverb

Study while others are sleeping; work while others are loafing; prepare while others are playing; and dream while others are wishing.
William Arthur Ward

All men who have achieved great things have been great dreamers.
Orison Swett Marden

Dreams are extremely important. You can't do it unless you imagine it.
George Lucas

Dreams come true. Without that possibility, nature would not incite us to have them.
John Updike

Dreams are good. Realities are better.
American Express

If you can't make a mistake, you can't make anything.
Marva Collins

I do not want to die…until I have faithfully made the most of my talent and cultivated the seed that was placed in me until the last small twig has grown.
Kathe Kollwitz

You'll never achieve your dreams if they don't become goals.
Anonymous

Twenty years from now you will be more disappointed by the things that you didn't do than by the ones you did do. So throw off the bowlines. Sail away from the safe harbor. Catch the trade winds in your sails. Explore. Dream. Discover.
Mark Twain

Don't wait for something big to occur. Start where you are, with what you have, and that will always lead you into something greater.
Mary Manin Morrissey

The things that one most wants to do are the things that are probably most worth doing.
Winifred Holtby

I've come to believe that each of us has a personal calling thats as unique as a fingerprint - and that the best way to succeed is to discover what you love and then find a way to offer it to others in the form of service, working hard, and also allowing the energy of the universe to lead you.
Oprah Winfrey

Before you begin a thing, remind yourself that difficulties and delays quite impossible to foresee are ahead. If you could see them clearly, naturally you could do a great deal to get rid of them but you can't. You can only see one thing clearly and that is your goal. Form a mental vision of that and cling to it through thick and thin.
Kathleen Norris

It takes a lot of courage to show your dreams to someone else.
Erma Bombeck

If one advances confidently in the direction of his dreams, and endeavors to live the life which he has imagined, he will meet with a success unexpected in common hours.
Henry David Thoreau

No dream comes true until you wake up and go to work.
Anonymous

The key to realizing a dream is to focus not on success but significance - and then even the small steps and little victories along your path will take on greater meaning.
Oprah Winfrey

Always chase your dreams instead of running from your fears.
Unknown Author

block your dream when you allow your fear to grow bigger than your faith.
Mary Manin Morrissey

The reason most people never reach their goals is that they don't define them, or ever seriously consider them as believable or achievable. Winners can tell you where they are going, what they plan to do along the way, and who will be sharing the adventure with them.
Denis Watley

You face the biggest challenge of all: to have the courage to seek your big dream regardless of what anyone says. You are the only person alive who can see your big picture and even you can't see it all.
Oprah Winfrey

Decisions

> What you decide on will be done, and
> light will shine on your ways.
> **Job 22:28**

A decision is the outcome of careful consideration among a set of options. When you begin the decision-making process, you start with an objective. What is the desired outcome? Once the outcome is defined, you begin the process of determining potential options and scenarios that will allow you to reach the objective. Identifying solutions is the point where people tend to have the most difficulty. It is easy to know what you ultimately want to achieve. It is the distance between point A and point C that poses the problem. It is also fairly easy to define options and scenarios. The problem is that each option is like a tree with branches. One option leads to another tree with branches. One scenario leads to another set of branches. Before you know it, the two or three scenarios you started with have branched out into two or three more scenarios with multiple scenarios each. The challenge is to not go so far down the branches that you become tangled in all of the options. When people cannot seem to make a decision, this is typically the reason. They have become overwhelmed with the number of options to consider before making the decision.

Sometimes you just have to take the leap. A friend phoned recently and shared with me a calling on her life to work with children. Children are naturally drawn to her wherever she goes, whether at the park or the grocery store. Though we have been good friends for several years, I never knew she had a dream of owning a day care center. As we were talking, she mentioned a dream she'd had. She was amazed because in this dream God told her to prepare a business plan for the day care.

Ten years had passed since she had thought about starting a day care business. Yet in the dream God gave her the name of the day care center, the location, and the timing. It happens the location was the same piece of land she had been driving past for two years.

While my friend was excited about the confirmation from God, she immediately became fearful and unsure of her next steps. Her first thought was, "Does God really give specific time frames?" Her second thought was, "But I don't want to quit my corporate job on this timing." I gave her two responses.

First, God's timing is perfect, whether it's the timing you expected or not. One Sunday morning Bishop Michael Dantley of Christ Emmanuel Church in Walnut Hills, Ohio, was teaching from the sixth chapter in the book of Joshua regarding the fall of the walls of Jericho. If you read the chapter, you will see that God decreed the fall of the walls seven days before it happened. God told Joshua the city was already his to possess and proceeded to give him specific instructions to claim the city. Once God gave Joshua instructions, it was up to Joshua to take action. Joshua followed God's specific instructions to march around the city in silence once each day for six days. On the seventh day, Joshua, the priests, and the people circled the city again. At Joshua's command, the priests blew the trumpets, the people gave a mighty shout, and the walls of the city crumpled.

What God declared came to pass because Joshua acted on the promise. He made a decision to act. This principle holds true today. When God gives you a vision and you make the decision to act on it, success follows. The success will not necessarily come easily, but God is willing to do his part once you commit. As Bishop Dantley stated, "God's people have to walk into God's declaration. God speaks what will happen, but in his mind, it has already happened."

Secondly, do not be deterred by barriers. You often miss opportunities because you create obstacles before you even begin. Another friend reminds me of this all the time. I am a closet inventor. I often come up with ideas and later realize some of them are already patented. The last time this happened I was discouraged, and then she said something very enlightening: "There may also be a patent on shoes, but a lot of folks sell them."

Just because the idea is not original does not mean there is no opportunity. You just have to think outside of the box. For my friend with the dream of owning a day care, I shared that there was no rule that said she had to be an on-site day care owner. She could continue to work her corporate job and act as an absentee owner. There were a number of different options. The key was to proceed with developing the business plan and define those details as she went.

As a friend, I intervened before she could begin swirling in indecision. I sent her a business plan template and said, "Get started." Too much focus on the details before starting leads to indecision and no progress. You have likely heard the term "analysis paralysis." This is what occurs when you become so bogged down in the data that you cannot make a decision. In effect, you become paralyzed by details and never move forward without external intervention. Considerable thought should indeed be given when making great decisions. However, you must be careful not to become so mired in the details that you make no progress toward the goal.

There are several types of people. There are people who talk about what *could* be done…if someone else would do it. There are lots of people who talk about what *should* be done…if someone else would just do it. There are far fewer people who actually *do* what can be done. These are the people who say, "I will just do it myself." Which one are you?

> If you limit your choices only to what seems possible
> or reasonable, you disconnect yourself from what you
> truly want, and all that is left is a compromise.
> **Robert Fritz**

> Choice, not circumstances, determines your success.
> **Unknown Author**

> You control your future, your destiny. What you think about comes about. By recording your dreams and goals on paper, you set in motion the process of becoming the person you most want to be. Put your future in good hands - your own.
> **Mark Victor Hansen**

> An executive is a person who always decides; sometimes
> he decides correctly, but he always decides.
> **John H. Patterson**

> Thinking is easy, acting is difficult, and to put one's thoughts
> into action is the most difficult thing in the world.
> **Johann Wolfgang von Goethe**

Don't wait until everything is just right. It will never be perfect. There will always be challenges, obstacles and less than perfect conditions. So what. Get started now. With each step you take, you will grow stronger and stronger, more and more skilled, more and more self-confident and more and more successful.
Mark Victor Hansen

If you send up a weather vane or put your thumb up in the air every time you want to do something different, to find out what people are going to think about it, you're going to limit yourself. That's a very strange way to live.
Jessye Norman

It is hard to imagine a more stupid or more dangerous way of making decisions than by putting those decisions in the hands of people who pay no price for being wrong.
Thomas Sowell

The indispensable first step to getting the things you want out of life is this: Decide what you want.
Ben Stein

Change

> He changes times and seasons;
> he sets up kings and deposes them.
> He gives wisdom to the wise
> and knowledge to the discerning.
> **Daniel 2:21**

You have been living in the same small town all of your life. You have had the same group of friends since high school. You have worked at the same job for twenty years. Is this all there is? It does not have to be. There is so much more if you choose to make changes. You just have to take a step. You have not moved to a new city and you have not changed jobs because staying put is safe. You are in your comfort zone. There is no need to learn how to interact with new people because you already have your set of friends, right? There is no need for you to change careers because you are comfortable at the same company where you have worked for twenty years, right? You know the job. You know the people. You know what is expected of you. You get a steady paycheck. What more could you ask for?

What is change? The Encarta World English Dictionary defines change as follows:

1. **become or make different:** to become different, or make something or somebody different
2. **substitute or replace something:** to exchange, substitute, or replace something
3. **pass from one state to another:** to pass or make something pass from one state or stage to another

The idea of changing from what or where you are today to a state that is unknown is why people fear change. Dr. A. J. Schuler, an expert in leadership and organizational change, details her "top ten reasons people resist change":

1. *The risk of change is seen as greater than the risk of standing still.*

I have worked for several companies over the course of my career. As a result of those various experiences, I have a healthy respect and need for change. In the majority of the companies I have worked for, the employees have come from a variety of backgrounds. The one exception is Procter and Gamble. P&G is a company that hires the majority of its employees directly from college or acquisitions. These employees grow up within the company, identifying with its processes and establishing lifelong friendships. Unlike employees in other companies, P&G employees do not typically leave the company. They know P&G so well they believe the risk of leaving is greater than remaining in their current environment.

2. *People feel connected to other people who are identified with the old way.*

Faith to Conquer Fear

My husband and I lived in Florida during the first two years of our marriage. As our first move from our North Carolina home, we naturally migrated to the same AME church denomination we already knew when we chose a new church. During that time, we established new friendships and became active in the church. As time progressed, however, we realized we were not aligned to the views of the leadership of the church we were attending. In hindsight, we recognized that we had not conducted our search for the right church with due diligence. In our eagerness to quickly find a church, we did not properly evaluate all aspects of the church aside from the friendly people. When we realized the church was not the ideal place for us, we were so entrenched with the friendships and the African Methodist Episcopal way that we just stayed until my company relocated us to another location.

3. *People have no role models for the new activity.*

Founded in 1996, *Dress for Success* is a nonprofit organization designed to help disadvantaged women enter or return to the workforce. It is most widely known for providing suits to women to enable them to make a positive first impression in job interviews. It is very easy to tell someone, "You need to be professional." However, if that person has no concept of what professional looks like or does not have the means to polish her appearance, she will not likely be able to make the change. In order to *be* professional, she needs to *see* professional.

Dress for Success has since expanded its services to include a career center that provides career guidance in the form of interviewing preparation and resume writing. The nonprofit also offers networking and mentoring opportunities to disadvantaged women via its Professional Women's Group. *Dress for Success* is a phenomenal organization and a great example of how role modeling can effect change.

4. *People fear they lack the competence to change.*

Competence and confidence are interchangeable in this scenario. A lack of self-confidence increases the belief that you are not competent enough to make the change. I have a friend who is a single parent with three children. She has struggled to make ends meet for years. Recently, she had an opportunity to leverage her ability to speak Spanish to get a better job that paid significantly higher wages than her current position. She has yet to apply. What is her logic? I believe it is a combination of fear of change and lack of self-confidence in her ability to change her circumstances.

5. *People feel overloaded and overwhelmed.*

My husband has decided he wants to be a school teacher. He is completing an online degree after being out of school for seventeen years. He is currently taking a math course, which is causing us much distress. The challenge is that he is attempting to solve the math problems the way he used to do it versus embracing the new way. This is causing him to work harder to complete the tasks because he does not clearly remember the old way of doing the math, but he is also not clear on the new techniques. He is doing double the work in an attempt to reconcile both his old knowledge and new learning. He is overloaded and overwhelmed because the course covers material he learned over twenty years ago. In his mind the math equations look familiar, but the terminology is unfamiliar. There is a merging of the old and the new. The stress of the need to do well, coupled with the quick pace of the course, is causing resistance to adapt to the new methods.

6. *People have a healthy skepticism and want to be sure new ideas are sound.*

When new ideas or innovation appears, consumers naturally divide themselves into innovators, early adopters, early majority, late adopters, and laggards through the process of diffusion.

Wikipedia defines Diffusion of Innovations as "a theory of how, why and at what rate new ideas and technology spread through cultures." This adoption process among people works the same whether the new concept is a product or a change in company policy. The rate at which people embrace the new idea is consistent.

Innovators are among the first 2.5 percent of the market to try a new product. These are the people who are always on the lookout for the next great thing. They preorder the product and wait in line to purchase. These individuals are risk takers. They tend to be young and to socialize with like-minded innovators.

Early adopters are among the earliest consumers to try a new product. They typically represent approximately 13.5 percent of a market. These consumers are usually younger and well educated. Early adopters also tend to have the highest degree of marketplace influence. Innovators and early adopters are the best groups for companies to target when marketing new ideas and innovation.

Early majority take significantly longer to adopt a new idea as compared to the innovators or early adopters. However, they still have a sphere of influence. Because they tend to have more contact with early adopters, that connection exposes them to the new concepts sooner.

Late adopters are very skeptical of anything new. The majority of consumers have adopted the new product long before they are willing to try it for themselves. Late adopters are not considered thought leaders and are prone to socializing with other late and early adopters.

Laggards are the last to adopt a new innovation or process. These consumers do not like change and therefore will not likely be the ones to lead or immediately align to change. Laggards like tradition and doing things "the way we've always done it." They tend to be more advanced in age and socialize predominantly with family and close friends.

Which of these are you when it comes to change?

7. *People fear hidden agendas among would-be reformers.*

In the Old Testament, there were strict processes to be followed in order to ask God for forgiveness, make atonement for sins, and offer thanks for God's blessings. Burnt offerings, grain offerings, drink offerings, animal sacrifices, and first fruit offerings were common practice. People had to rely on the Levitical priests to pray to God on their behalf. The priests could only pray for the people once a year by entering into the Holy of Holies within the inner sanctuary of the Tabernacle. But once Jesus was born, everything changed.

Jesus Christ was a reformer. He taught His followers how to pray for themselves and speak directly to the Father through the Lord's Prayer. Sacrifices and offerings were no longer needed for the forgiveness of sins. He taught that belief in him was the way to gain salvation, not through the Levitical priests. Although God gave Moses the Ten Commandments, Jesus Christ was the living example of the Ten Commandments in action. As a consequence of his teachings, Jesus was persecuted by the government, hated by the established church, and ultimately crucified.

8. *People feel the proposed change threatens their notions of themselves.*

The Civil Rights Movement (1955–1968) was a movement in the United States aimed at ending racial discrimination against African Americans. Before the Civil Rights Movement, restaurants, bathrooms, movie theaters, water fountains, buses, and the like were segregated. Blacks were required to enter through separate doors. Black people could not sit in the same section of the movie theaters and had to sit in the balcony while white patrons sat on the lower level in premium seats. Blacks had to sit in the back of the bus even if there were seats available in the front just because of skin color. At that time, this was the norm. Whites were accustomed to special treatment, and blacks were accustomed to inferior and partial treatment.

The Civil Rights Movement changed both white and black people's notions of themselves. Nonviolent acts of protest such as the Montgomery Bus Boycott incited by Rosa Parks and the Greensboro sit-in paved the way for long-term changes for the equality of blacks and other minorities in the South. These acts led to legislature such as the Civil Rights Act of 1964, which banned discrimination based on religion, race, national origin, or color in employment practices or public accommodations. The Voting Rights Act of 1965 restored and protected voting rights by outlawing discriminatory voting practices based on race or color. The Immigration and Nationality Services Act of 1965 allowed entry of immigrants to the United States. The Fair Housing Act of 1968 banned discrimination in the sale or rental of housing.

The Civil Rights Movement prompted the type of change that caused people to question their lifelong beliefs. There was significant resistance to the movement and what it meant to the future of both minorities and whites in the South.

9. *People anticipate a loss of status or quality of life.*

In the books of Genesis and Exodus in the Bible, Joseph, the son of Jacob, found favor with Pharaoh, the king of Egypt. With the help of God, Joseph was able to interpret a dream for Pharaoh that none other in Egypt could interpret. The dream foretold the seven years of feast and the seven years of famine for Egypt.

While Pharaoh and Joseph lived, the people of Israel lived a good life and increased in numbers. However, once Joseph died and a new king who did not know Joseph was appointed, the Israelites' quality of life changed. The new king determined that the Israelites were living better than the Egyptians, so he assigned taskmasters to institute slavery. The Israelites endured hard labor and harsh treatment as they worked making bricks and laboring in the fields.

After four hundred thirty years in bondage, God worked through Moses and Aaron to convince Pharaoh to release the Israelites from slavery so that they could leave Egypt. When God delivered the people of Israel out of Egypt, they spent forty years in the wilderness. Initially the people rejoiced and were grateful to God for their deliverance, and God provided for their physical needs. Manna rained from heaven every morning for forty years. Their only requirement was to go outside every morning and pick up enough manna to feed their families each day. They did not even have to work for the food.

When the Israelites complained about only receiving manna, God sent quails in the evening for meat. Every need was being met, yet they still murmured and grumbled about the change. In Numbers 11:5, the people complained that back in Egypt they had their fill of fish, cucumbers, melons, leeks, onions, and garlic. Yet in the wilderness they only had manna. How quickly they forgot about the harsh conditions of slavery they endured. Slavery was a high price to pay for fish and cucumbers. Despite this, in their minds, their quality of life had been adversely affected.

10. *People genuinely believe that the proposed change is a bad idea.*

When there is a change, try to remain open-minded. Can you figure out what bothers you most about it? Is it how the change is being implemented? Do you agree with the outcome but not the process? As with the options on a GPS, acknowledge that there is more than one way to reach a particular destination.

Each of these reasons has likely resonated with you at some point in your personal or work life. However, you will find that you are able to embrace a change when it supports your goals or values. Once you assess the importance of the change and understand that it will ultimately help to achieve your goals, it becomes an easier process.

It takes a lot of courage to release the familiar and seemingly secure, to embrace the new. But there is no real security in what is no longer meaningful. There is more security in the adventurous and exciting, for in movement there is life, and in change there is power.
Alan Cohen

I found every single successful person I've ever spoken to had a turning point. The turning point was when they made a clear, specific unequivocal decision that they were not going to live like this anymore; they were going to achieve success. Some people make that decision at 15 and some people make it at 50, and most people never make it all.
Brian Tracy

It's not so much that we're afraid of change or so in love with the old ways, but it's that place in between that we fear…Its like being between trapezes. Its Linus when his blanket is in the dryer. There's nothing to hold on to.
Marilyn Ferguson

If you don't like where you are, then change it! You are not a tree.
Jim Rohn

Change will not come if we wait for some other person or some other time. We are the ones we've been waiting for. We are the change that we seek.
Barack Obama

The jump is so frightening between where I am and where I want to be…because of all I may become I will close my eyes and leap.
Mary Ann Radmacher

Christy L. Demetrakis

If you don't like something, change it. If you can't change it, change your attitude. Don't complain.
Maya Angelou

Talent

The Parable of the Talents

[14]"Again, it will be like a man going on a journey, who called his servants and entrusted his property to them. [15]To one he gave five talents of money, to another two talents, and to another one talent, each according to his ability. Then he went on his journey. [16]The man who had received the five talents went at once and put his money to work and gained five more. [17]So also, the one with the two talents gained two more. [18]But the man who had received the one talent went off, dug a hole in the ground and hid his master's money.
[19]"After a long time the master of those servants returned and settled accounts with them. [20]The man who had received the five talents brought the other five. 'Master,' he said, 'you entrusted me with five talents. See, I have gained five more.'
[21]"His master replied, 'Well done, good and faithful servant! You have been faithful with a few things; I will put you in charge of many things. Come and share your master's happiness!'
[22]"The man with the two talents also came. 'Master,' he said, 'you entrusted me with two talents; see, I have gained two more.'

[23]"His master replied, 'Well done, good and faithful servant! You have been faithful with a few things; I will put you in charge of many things. Come and share your master's happiness!'
[24]"Then the man who had received the one talent came. 'Master,' he said, 'I knew that you are a hard man, harvesting where you have not sown and gathering where you have not scattered seed. [25]So I was afraid and went out and hid your talent in the ground. See, here is what belongs to you.'
[26]"His master replied, 'You wicked, lazy servant! So you knew that I harvest where I have not sown and gather where I have not scattered seed? [27]Well then, you should have put my money on deposit with the bankers, so that when I returned I would have received it back with interest.
[28]"Take the talent from him and give it to the one who has the ten talents. [29]For everyone who has will be given more, and he will have an abundance. Whoever does not have, even what he has will be taken from him."

Matthew 25:14-29

There is a parable in the Bible found in 2 Kings 4 about a widow and her two sons:

The Widow's Oil

[1]The wife of a man from the company of the prophets cried out to Elisha, "Your servant my husband is dead, and you know that he revered the LORD. But now his creditor is coming to take my two boys as his slaves."

Faith to Conquer Fear

²Elisha replied to her, "How can I help you? Tell me, what do you have in your house?" "Your servant has nothing there at all," she said, "except a little oil." ³Elisha said, "Go around and ask all your neighbors for empty jars. Don't ask for just a few. ⁴Then go inside and shut the door behind you and your sons. Pour oil into all the jars, and as each is filled, put it to one side." ⁵She left him and afterward shut the door behind her and her sons. They brought the jars to her and she kept pouring. ⁶When all the jars were full, she said to her son, "Bring me another one." But he replied, "There is not a jar left." Then the oil stopped flowing. ⁷She went and told the man of God, and he said, "Go, sell the oil and pay your debts. You and your sons can live on what is left."

2 Kings 4:1–7

The woman in this story was a widow. Her husband was the family's financial provider. After his death, there was no longer any money coming into the home. To collect on the debts that the family had, her deceased husband's creditors were going to take her two remaining sons as slaves. The woman pleaded with the prophet Elisha to help her. He asked the question, "What do you have in your house?" She replied, "Nothing there at all ... except a little oil." She was so focused on what she did not have that she could not see what she did have to offer to help pay off her debts. Elisha instructed her to use what she had, the oil, and then to go out and ask for what she needed, the jars to fill with oil. His point was for the woman to take what God has already provided and then add to that by soliciting help from others.

Are you like this widow? Do you think that your skills are not enough to reach what has been placed on your heart to accomplish? If God has placed a dream in your spirit, then He has already given you a measure of the talent that you need to accomplish it. A talent is a skill that comes very easily to you. You are a natural, as they say. You have to believe that each person was placed on this earth for a specific purpose and destiny. God already knows what your talent and purpose is, even when you are still searching to figure it out for yourself.

Your talent is likely very obvious to everyone except you. If you are unsure of your strengths, ask friends and family for input. Ask them what they think you are good at or what skills they have observed in you that sets you apart from others. After hearing from a number of people, look for the similarities. The one or two areas that are consistent are probably your predominant talent. What do you do that makes others say, "How did you do that so quickly" or "You make that look so easy"? That's your talent. What gifts and talents do you already possess that you can use right now to make your dream a reality?

> There are two kinds of talent, man-made talent and God-given talent. With man-made talent you have to work very hard. With God-given talent, you just touch it up once in a while.
> **Pearl Bailey**

> You are the only one who can use your ability.
> It is an awesome responsibility.
> **Zig Ziglar**

> Hide not your talents, they for use were made. What's a sun-dial in the shade?
> **Benjamin Franklin**

> Use what talents you possess: the woods would be very silent if no birds sang there except those that sang best.
> **Henry Van Dyke**

> Whatever you are by nature, keep to it; never desert your line of talent. Be what nature intended you for and you will succeed.
> **Sydney Smith**

If you have a talent, use it in every which way possible. Don't hoard it. Don't dole it out like a miser. Spend it lavishly like a millionaire intent on going broke.
Brendan Francis Behan

Work while you have the light. You are responsible for the talent that has been entrusted to you.
Henri Frederic Amiel

Communication

Do not let any unwholesome talk come out of your mouths, but only what is helpful for building others up according to their needs, that it may benefit those who listen.
Ephesians 4:29

Communication is the process of expressing a want, thought, need, or desire to someone. There are three different types of communication: written, verbal, and nonverbal. Both humans and animals use a combination of these types of communication to achieve their goals. People use it to persuade influence, express, humor, confuse, describe, and empower...to name a few. Communication influences people either positively or negatively.

It is important to recognize your own communication style. I am a very direct communicator. As such, I believe in speaking and writing without a lot of fluff. My language is not flowery, and my statements tend to be brief.

A direct communication style is both a blessing and a curse. If you are speaking with a person with a similar communication style, it works well. On the other hand, if you are communicating with a person who has a more descriptive language and likes to take their time getting to the point, you may be perceived as too aggressive.

Whether a specific communication style is effective or not depends on the environment. Your communication style may and should vary depending on the setting and the audience. I have had the wonderful opportunity to work for several Fortune 500 companies over the course of my career. The culture and communication styles are different by company. Some companies rely heavily on e-mail. Others are more reliant on voice mail and face-to-face meetings.

The Gillette Company, before it was acquired by P&G had a culture of direct communication. Issues were handled directly without numerous meetings to reach resolution. Comparatively, at Procter and Gamble, collaboration is highly valued. Meetings to reach consensus are commonplace. Bad news is shared in a positive manner. Direct communication is not the norm. There is a language all its own that can only be learned by being an active student. P&G has created a culture of collaboration over the years that can be both effective and ineffective, depending on how quickly decisions need to be made.

Communication styles are as diverse as people are. The best companies have determined that leveraging diversity improves overall business results. Diversity brings fresh, new perspectives to old business issues. Communication diversity can be an advantage as well. No one type of communication style is most effective in every situation. As the communicator, ensure you are aware of the environment and the most effective way to communicate to achieve the desired results.

To effectively communicate, we must realize that we are all different in the way we perceive the world and use this understanding as a guide to our communication with others.
Tony Robbins

When people talk, listen completely. Most people never listen.
Ernest Hemingway

To listen well is as powerful a means of communication and influence as to talk well.
John Marshall

It's so simple to be wise. Just think of something stupid to say and then don't say it.
Sam Levenson

Be sincere; be brief; be seated.
Franklin Delano Roosevelt

Many attempts to communicate are nullified by saying too much.
Robert Greenleaf

Wise men talk because they have something to say; fools, because they have to say something.
Plato

If you'd think 1% more, you'd speak 50% less, and appear 100% more intelligent.
Scott Sorrell

Drawing on my fine command of the English language, I said nothing.
Robert Benchley

It's good to shut up sometimes.
Marcel Marceau

I quote others in order to better express my own self.
Michel de Montaigne

I wish people who have trouble communicating would just shut up.
Tom Lehrer

If I am to speak ten minutes, I need a week for preparation; if fifteen minutes, three days; if half an hour, two days; if an hour, I am ready now.
Woodrow Wilson

It is not so much the content of what one says as the way in which one says it. However important the thing you say, what's the good of it if not heard or, being heard, not felt.
Sylvia Ashton-Warner

Effective communication is 20% what you know and 80% how you feel about what you know.
Jim Rohn

Success

> For I know the plans I have for you," declares the LORD, "plans to prosper you and not to harm you, plans to give you hope and a future."
> **Jeremiah 29:11**

Success is a combination of strategy and execution. Strategy can be defined as the key focus areas for attaining an overall vision. Procter and Gamble has a corporate vision of "improving the everyday lives of the world's consumers and the communities in which we live and work." As a for-profit company, P&G also has a vision of consistent growth within the consumer products industry. If you reference P&G's 2009 annual report, chairman of the board A. G. Lafley shared the three strategies that drove the majority of P&G's growth over the last ten years:

1. Focused on the core business and leading billion-dollar brands, to win with the biggest and strongest retail customers and the most important countries.
2. Shifted focus of the business portfolio to faster-growing, more asset-efficient and higher- margin businesses.
3. Improved the affordability and availability of P&G brands to low-income consumers, with an emphasis on developing markets.

Those were the strategies. The detailed execution of these strategies was what led to the positive sales growth the company experienced in the last decade.

Execution is the accomplishment of the tactics or actions that support the strategy. A strategy is useless if not executed properly. P&G leverages its wealth of assets to execute its strategies. The company's biggest asset is its employees. P&G relies on its employees to create the strategy, develop the tactics, and execute the strategy. Their success is dependent on good strategy and great execution. They have an excellent track record of delivering innovation and products that appeal to a broad range of consumers. Failure is not an option for a company the size of Procter and Gamble. Both the company and its employees have a mind-set that does not consider failure.

Internationally acclaimed author and lecturer Marianne Williamson said, "Our deepest fear is not that we are inadequate. Our deepest fear is that we are powerful beyond measure. It is our light, not our darkness, that most frightens us." I challenge you to think about what you really fear. It seems counterintuitive to want something and then have fear of actually achieving it. Do you want more out of life? Do you want to spend the rest of your life wondering how successful you might have been? Analyze your current environment. Is it conducive to your success? Sometimes people and circumstances have to change in order to position you for success. Can you achieve the success you envision where you are? You may get discouraged, but you must be willing to endure some trials to be successful. You must be willing to change your environment.

Lonnie Johnson, an aerospace engineer, invented the Super Soaker. Though squirt guns existed prior to his invention, his creation, originally known as the Power Drencher, was the first water blaster to incorporate air pressure into its design. Johnson came up with the idea of the Super Soaker completely by accident. In 1982, a nozzle at his bathroom sink shot a spray of water across the room. That occurrence was the inspiration for the inventor to create a pressurized water gun. Let's consider the timeline. Lonnie Johnson had the idea in 1982. He spent six years developing the prototype. Around 1988, he began the patent process for his invention. It took three years for him to receive the patent. Several manufacturers declined the opportunity to make and market the Super Soaker before Larami Corporation agreed to take on the idea. Since 1990, over 40 million Super Soakers have been sold, with sales of over $200 million. It took Lonnie Johnson ten years from idea to manufacturing with numerous challenges along the way. However, he persevered and continues to reap benefits.

Marion Donovan was the inventor of the disposable diaper. As a child, Marion learned much of her innovative skills from her father and uncle. When Marion became a mother, she struggled with the common issue all mothers faced: cloth diapers. Her first invention, in 1946, was a waterproof diaper cover designed to minimize the messes associated with leaking cloth diapers. This first invention was well received and was an instant success in 1949. She received a patent in 1951. In the meantime, Donovan was also working on the disposable paper diaper. While you may not believe it today given the popularity of disposable diapers, Marion Donovan did not have immediate success with this creation. She spent ten years shopping her idea around to major U.S. paper companies before Victor Mills, the creator of Pampers capitalized on her idea.

Take a minute to brainstorm all of the potential outcomes if you succeed and what the repercussions will be if you fail to deliver. Write them down. One of two things will happen. Either the potential successes will outweigh the negatives or the potential failures will outweigh the potential for success. Remember Abraham Lincoln's story in the chapter on determination? If Honest Abe had quit after his numerous defeats, history would have been changed forever.

Bishop T. D. Jakes, one of the most popular Christian preachers of our time, of The Potter's House in Dallas, Texas, ministered in a series on prosperity that success is intentional. "Nobody succeeds by accident. It is a process. If you have a plan and are working that plan, you know what levels of success you plan to achieve. There is no reason to be cautious. Are you planning to succeed or are you planning to fail? Either way, it's your plan."

> There are no secrets to success. It is the result of preparation, hard work, and learning from failure.
> **Colin Powell**

> To dream anything that you want to dream, that's the beauty of the human mind. To do anything that you want to do, that is the strength of the human will. To trust yourself to test your limits, that is the courage to succeed.
> **Bernard Edmonds**

> Limits, like fears, are often just an illusion.
> **Michael Jordan**

> I used to want the words "She tried" on my tombstone. Now I want "She did it."
> **Katherine Dunham**

Faith to Conquer Fear

When a man feels throbbing within him the power
to do what he undertakes as well as it can possibly
be done, this is happiness, this is success.
Orison Swett Marden

The great successful men of the world have used their
imagination ... they think ahead and create their mental picture
in all its details, filling in here, adding a little there, altering this
a bit and that a bit, but steadily building - steadily building.
Robert Collier

A man can fail many times, but he isn't a failure
until he begins to blame somebody else.
John Burroughs

Striving for success without hard work is like
trying to harvest where you haven't planted.
David Bly

If at first you do succeed try not to look too surprised.
Unknown Author

The greatest barrier to success is the fear of failure.
Sven Goran Eriksson

The best way to succeed in this world is to
act on the advice you give to others.
Unknown Author

You have to expect things of yourself before you can do them.
Michael Jordan

The secret of success in life is for a man to be
ready for his opportunity when it comes.
Benjamin Disraeli

Success is to be measured not so much by the position
that one has reached in life as by the obstacles which
he has overcome while trying to succeed.
Booker T. Washington

I don't know the key to success, but the key
to failure is trying to please everybody.
Bill Cosby

You know you are on the road to success if you
would do your job, and not be paid for it.
Oprah Winfrey

Many of life's failures are people who did not realize
how close they were to success when they gave up.
Thomas A. Edison

Aim for success, not perfection. Never give up your right
to be wrong, because then you will lose the ability to
learn new things and move forward with your life.
Dr. David M. Burns

Real success is finding your lifework in the work that you love.
David McCullough

Unless you choose to do great things with
it, it makes no difference how much you are
rewarded, or how much power you have.
Oprah Winfrey

My mother drew a distinction between achievement and success. She said that achievement is the knowledge that you have studied and worked hard and done the best that is in you. Success is being praised by others, and that's nice, too, but not as important or satisfying. Always aim for achievement and forget about success.'
Helen Hayes

If your success is not on your own terms, if it looks good to the world but does not feel good in your heart, it is not success at all.
Anna Quindlen

Charge less, but charge. Otherwise, you will not be taken seriously, and you do your fellow artists no favors if you undercut the market.
Elizabeth Aston

Getting ahead in a difficult profession requires avid faith in yourself. That is why some people with mediocre talent, but with great inner drive, go much further than people with vastly superior talent.
Sophia Loren

Believe in yourself! Have faith in your abilities! Without a humble but reasonable confidence in your own powers you cannot be successful or happy.
Norman Vincent Peale

Often we don't even realize who we're meant to be because we're so busy trying to live out someone else's ideas. But other people and their opinions hold no power in defining our destiny.
Oprah Winfrey

Success is not the key to happiness. Happiness is the key to success. If you love what you are doing, you will be successful.
Herman Cain

Success means having the courage, the determination, and the will to become the person you believe you were meant to be.
George Sheehan

The greatest form of maturity is at harvest time. That is when we must learn how to reap without complaint if the amounts are small and how to reap without apology if the amounts are big.
Jim Rohn

In order to succeed, your desire for success should be greater than your fear of failure.
Bill Cosby

Success is a state of mind. If you want success, start thinking of yourself as a success.
Dr. Joyce Brothers

You can have everything in life you want, if you will just help other people get what they want.
Zig Ziglar

God gives every bird a worm, but he does not throw it into the nest.
Swedish Proverb

The Lord gave us two ends -- one to sit on and the other to think with. Success depends on which one we use the most.
Ann Landers

When we do more than what we are paid to do, eventually we will be paid more for what we do.
Richard Denny

If you don't go after what you want, you'll never have it. If you don't ask, the answer is always no. If you don't step forward, you're always in the same place.
Nora Roberts

Every time you state what you want or believe, you're the first to hear it. It's a message to both you and others about what you think is possible. Don't put a ceiling on yourself.
Oprah Winfrey

Everything you need is already inside. Just do it.
Bill Bowerman

Epilogue

> The tongue has the power of life and death,
> and those who love it will eat its fruit.
> **Proverbs 18:21**

When people are unable to inspire themselves, they often look to others for inspiration. This inspiration can come in the form of the written word or the spoken word. The spoken word is an amazing thing. It has the power to inspire or degrade, to build self-esteem or demoralize. Millions of dollars and endless hours are spent each year attending motivational seminars, retreats, conventions, and church services in search of a word that will change our lives. In order to accomplish anything worthwhile, man has demonstrated the need to be inspired and motivated to take the first step. We rely on inspiration to sprout from church, self-help books, and the like. Inspiration and encouragement can flow from those closest to us. Everyone possesses the ability to inspire others.

The quotes in this book are from authors, motivational speakers, sales trainers, generals, artists, and others who, either through everyday conversation or formal speeches, have provided words of wisdom that have the potential to drive mental and behavioral change. The essence of *Faith to Conquer Fear* is best summed up with these quotes:

The only thing that stands between a man and what
he wants from life is often merely the will to try
it and the faith to believe that it is possible.
David Viscott

You gain strength, courage, and confidence by every
experience in which you really stop to look fear in the face.
You must do the thing which you think you cannot do.
Eleanor Roosevelt

You must accept that you might fail; then, if you
do your best and still don't win, at least you can be
satisfied that you've tried. If you don't accept failure
as a possibility, you don't set high goals, you don't
branch out, you don't try – you don't take the risk.
Rosalynn Carter

Prepare your mind to receive the best that life has to offer.
Ernest Holmes

You have to believe in yourself and build your faith to achieve success. Every experience you face along the journey is working for your good. Those experiences will give you the confidence to overcome fear, hesitation, and complacency. You may indeed fail in the attempt, but try again. Thomas Edison did not create the light bulb on the first attempt. Do not give up. Talk about that new business or endeavor as if it already exists and you will find yourself walking in that reality. Follow your dream. Let's get on with it!

About the Author

Christy Demetrakis is president and founder of The Empowered Speaker, a communication skills training company. She conducts public workshops and customized on-site programs for companies and organizations. She is a certified instructor for the Speakers Training Camp.

Christy has spent the last sixteen years working in Fortune 500 companies in sales and management. She has a bachelor's degree in speech communications and radio, television, and motion pictures from the University of North Carolina–Chapel Hill. She also has a master's degree in business administration.

Christy is married to James and lives in Kentucky with their two children and their dog.

Who's Quoted

Adams, Charles Kendall: American educator and historian

Ali, Muhammad: retired American boxer and three-time World Heavyweight Champion

Allen, Woody: comedian, actor, and director

American Express: credit card company

Amiel, Henri Frederic: Swiss philosopher, poet, and critic

Angelou, Maya: author, poet, historian, songwriter, playwright, dancer, stage and screen producer, director, performer, singer, and civil rights activist

Armstrong, Lance: a champion professional cyclist

Armstrong, T. Alan: author

Ashe, Arthur: first African American player to compete in the international sport of tennis at the highest level

Ashton-Warner, Sylvia: novelist, autobiographer, and educational pioneer from New Zealand

Aston, Elizabeth: author of *Mr. Darcy's Daughters*

Bailey, Pearl: composer, singer, and songwriter

Banks, Harry F.: an Allied soldier serving in the Canadian Army who may have been crucified with bayonets or combat knives on a barn door or a tree while fighting on the Western Front during World War I

Behan, Brendan Francis: Irish poet and author best known for his 1958 novel *Borstal Boy*

Bell, Alexander Graham: scientist, inventor, engineer, and innovator who is credited with inventing the first practical telephone

Bell, Lawrence: an American industrialist and founder of Bell Aircraft Corporation

Benchley, Robert: writer, critic, and film actor

Bennett, Bo: businessman, author, programmer, philanthropist, martial artist, motivational speaker, and amateur comedian

Berle, Milton: American comedian and actor

Bly, David: Minnesota District 25B state representative

Bombeck, Erma: novelist and columnist

Bowerman, Bill: track and field coach and founder of Nike, Inc.

Brothers, Joyce: psychologist, advice columnist, writer, and actress

Brown, H. Jackson, Jr.: *New York Times* best-selling author of *Life's Little Instruction Book*

Browne, Jackson: American rock singer-songwriter and musician

Burns, David M.: national best-selling author and medical doctor

Buscalgia, Leo F.: PhD, author, and University of Southern California professor

Cain, Herman: CEO and president of The New Voice, Inc., radio talk show host, and Fox News commentator

Carter, Jimmy: thirty-ninth president of the United States and the recipient of the 2002 Nobel Peace Prize (1977-1981)

Carter, Rosalynn: First Lady of the United States from 1977 to 1981 and a leading advocate for mental health research

Castro, Rick: American photographer, motion picture director, and stylist

Chambers, Oswald: early-twentieth century Scottish Protestant Christian minister and teacher, best known as the author of the widely read devotional *My Utmost for His Highest*

Checketts, Dave: American sports businessman serving in such roles as general manager of the Utah Jazz and president of the New York Knicks

Clegg, Graeme: motivational speaker in New Zealand and Asia

Cliffe, Albert E.: author of *Let Go and Let God*

Cohen, Alan: author of inspirational books and contributing writer for the *Chicken Soup for the Soul* series

Collier, Robert: writer and publisher of inspirational success books such as *The Secret of the Ages*

Collins, Marva: African American educator who started Westside Preparatory School in Garfield Park, an impoverished neighborhood of Chicago, Illinois, in 1975

Coolidge, John Calvin: thirtieth president of the United States of America (1923 – 1929)

Cosby, Bill: American comedian, actor, author, television producer, musician, and activist

Covey, Stephen: author, professional speaker, consultant, and management expert

Dantley, Michael E.: associate provost and associate vice president for Academic Affairs, senior pastor of Christ Emmanuel Christian Fellowship church in Cincinnati, Ohio

Davis, William Hersey: professor of New Testament interpretation at Southern Baptist Theological Seminary, 1920–1948

Demetrakis, Christy: author of *Faith to Conquer Fear: Inspiration to Achieve your Dreams*, public speaker and entrepreneur

Denny, Richard: inspirational public speaker in the UK

Disraeli, Benjamin: British prime minister, parliamentarian, conservative statesman, and author

Dumas, Mary O'Hare: author

Dunham, Katherine: African American dancer, choreographer, songwriter, author, educator, and activist

Edison, Thomas: American inventor, scientist, and businessman who developed many devices, including the phonograph, the motion picture camera, and a long-lasting, practical electric lightbulb, that greatly influenced life around the world

Edmonds, Bernard: priest, organ historian, photographer, and railway enthusiast

Eriksson, Sven Goran: director of football for Notts County Football Club in Nottingham, England

Ferguson, Marilyn: influential American author, editor, and public speaker, best known for her 1980 book *The Aquarian Conspiracy*

Fitzgerald, Ella: popular female jazz singer in the United States who was dubbed "The First Lady of Song"

Ford, Henry: American founder of the Ford Motor Company and father of modern assembly lines

France, Anatole: French poet, journalist, and novelist

Franklin, Benjamin: one of the Founding Fathers of the United States of America; also a leading author and printer, satirist, political theorist, politician, scientist, inventor, civic activist, statesman, soldier, and diplomat

Fritz, Robert: founder of Technologies for Creating®, composer, filmmaker, and organizational consultant

Gandhi, Mohandas Karanchand (a.k.a., Mahatma Gandhi): political and spiritual leader of India during the Indian independence movement

Gill, Vince: country music performer, musician, and songwriter

Goethe, Johann Wolfgang von: German writer whose works span the fields of poetry, drama, literature, theology, philosophy, humanism, and science.

Greenleaf, Robert: founder of the modern *Servant Leadership* movement

Hansen, Mark Victor: coauthor of *Chicken Soup for the Soul* and *The One Minute Millionaire* series

Hayes, Helen: American actress who garnered the nickname "First Lady of the American theatre"

Hemingway, Ernest: American writer and journalist known for his novella *The Old Man and the Sea*

High Eagle: Osage and Cherokee American Indian, composer, author, musician, and speaker

Hill, Napoleon: journalist, attorney, lecturer, and author of *Think and Grow Rich*

Hilton, Conrad: founder of the Hilton hotel chain

Holmes, Ernest: American writer and spiritual teacher; founder of the Religious Science movement

Holt, Jon: supporter of school reform; author of numerous books on educational theory and practice, children's rights, and alternative schooling

Holtby, Winifred: English journalist and novelist best known for the novel *South Riding*

Holtz, Lou: former football head coach, author, television commentator, and motivational speaker

Holy Bible: New International Version

Jacobi, Carl Gustav Jacob: Prussian mathematician

Jordan, Michael: retired American professional basketball player and businessman

Keller, James: Roman Catholic priest who founded The Christophers, a Christian inspirational group which broadcasts a weekly inspirational television show on ABC

Kemph, Richard: author

King, Martin Luther, Jr.: American clergyman, activist, and prominent leader in the African American civil rights movement

Kollwitz, Kathe: German expressionist printmaker and sculptor

L'Amour, Louis: American novelist and writer of primarily Western adventures

Landers, Ann: a pen name created in 1943 by *Chicago Sun-Times* columnist **Ruth Crowley,** whose syndicated advice column ran in many newspapers for fifty-six years

Lehrer, Tom: American singer-songwriter, satirist, pianist, and mathematician

Levenson, Sam: American humorist, writer, television host, and journalist

Lewis, Clive Staples: one of the intellectual giants of the twentieth century and arguably the most influential Christian writer of his day

Loren, Sophia: Italian actress and winner of an Academy Award and five Golden Globes

Lorimer, George Horace: former editor-in-chief of the *Saturday Evening Post* (1936)

Lowell, James Russell: American Romantic poet and author of *The Biglow Papers*.

Lucas, George: American film producer, screenwriter, director, and founder/chairman of Lucasfilm Ltd.

Mandino, Og: inspirational author of the best-selling book *The Greatest Salesman in the World*

Maravich, Pete (a.k.a., Pistol Pete): professional basketball player

Marceau, Marcel: French mime artist and actor

Marden, Orison Swett: American writer associated with the New Thought movement

Marshall, John: American statesman and jurist; the longest-serving chief justice in Supreme Court history

Maughan, W. Somerset: English playwright, novelist, and short story writer

McCullough, David: American author, narrator, lecturer, and two-time winner of the Pulitzer Prize

Montaigne, Michel de: one of the most influential writers of the French Renaissance; credited with popularizing the essay as a literary genre

Morley, Christopher: American journalist, novelist, essayist, and poet

Morrissey, Mary Manin: a New Thought minister from Oregon and the author of *Building Your Dreams* and *No Less Than Greatness*

Niebuhr, Reinhold: American theologian

Norman, Jessye: American opera singer and one of the highest-paid performers in classical music

Norris, Kathleen: best-selling poet and essayist best known for her writings about Christian spirituality

Obama, Barack: the forty-fourth president of the United States of America; the first African American to assume the office of president

Overton, Patrick: director of the Front Porch Institute in Astoria, Oregon, which focuses on nonprofit, community-based organizational development, facility assessment, strategic planning, cultural assessment, and cultural planning

Patterson, John H.: industrialist and founder of the National Cash Register Company

Peale, Norman Vincent: Protestant preacher and author of *The Power of Positive Thinking*

Plato: classical Greek philosopher, mathematician, writer of philosophical dialogues, and founder of the Academy in Athens, the first institution of higher learning in the Western world

Powell, Colin: American statesman and a retired four-star general in the United States Army; the sixty-fifth and first African American United States secretary of state (20012005), serving under president George W. Bush

Quindlen, Anna: author of five best-selling novels, six nonfiction books, and two children's books

Radmacher, Mary Anne: writer and artist

Ravn, Karen: author and contributor to the *Los Angeles Times*

Robbins, Tony: American self-help author and motivational speaker

Roberts, Nora: American author

Rohn, Jim: Motivational speaker, entrepreneur, and philosopher

Roosevelt, Eleanor: First from 1933 to 1945, and internationally prominent author, speaker, politician, and activist for the New Deal coalition

Roosevelt, Franklin Delano: thirty-second president of the United States of America (1933–1945)

Ruskin, John: English art critic, poet, and artist

Sandburg, Carl: American writer and editor; winner of three Pulitzer Prizes

Schwarzkopf, H. Norman: retired United States Army general who was commander of the Coalition Forces in the Gulf War of 1991

Seneca, Lucius Annaeus (a.k.a., Seneca the Younger): Roman Stoic philosopher, statesman, and drama playwright

Sheehan, George: author best known for his *New York Times* best-selling book, *Running & Being: The Total Experience*

Smith, Sydney: English writer and Anglican clergyman

Sorrell, Scott: professional sales trainer

Sowell, Thomas: senior fellow, Hoover Institute, Stanford University

St. Augustine: Romanized Berber philosopher and theologian; one of the most important figures in the development of Western Christianity

St. Thomas Aquinas: Italian priest of the Roman Catholic Church in the Dominican Order, an immensely influential philosopher and theologian in the tradition of scholasticism

Starr, Ralph Vaull: author

Stein, Ben: American actor, writer, and commentator on political and economic issues; Emmy Award winning game show host

Steinem, Gloria: American feminist, journalist, and social and political activist

Swindoll, Charles: Evangelical Christian pastor, author, educator, and radio preacher; senior pastor of Stonebriar Community Church, in Frisco, Texas

Thoreau, Henry David: American author, poet, naturalist, development critic, surveyor, historian, philosopher, and leading transcendentalist best known for his essay; *Civil Disobedience*

Tibolt, Frank: writer, motivator, and success trainer

Tracy, Brian: self-help author and the chairman of Brian Tracy International, a human resource company

Tubman, Harriet: runaway slave from Maryland led hundreds of slaves to freedom along the Underground Railroad; known as the "Moses of her people"

Twain, Mark: American author and humorist most noted for his novels *Adventures of Huckleberry Finn* and *The Adventures of Tom Sawyer*

Updike, John: American novelist, poet, short story writer, and art and literary critic

Valery, Paul: French poet, essayist, and philosopher

Van Dyke, Henry: American author, educator, and clergyman

Viscott, David: American psychiatrist, author, businessman, and media personality

Von Goethe, Johann Wolfgang: German writer whose works span the fields of poetry, drama, literature, theology, philosophy, humanism, and science.

Ward, William Arthur: author of *Fountains of Faith*

Washington, Booker T.: educator, author, and African American civil rights leader

Watley, Denis: author of *The Psychology of Success (Ten Proven Principles for Winning)*

Wilson, Woodrow: twenty-eighth president of the United States (1913–1921)

Winfrey, Oprah: American television host, producer, and philanthropist; best known for *The Oprah Winfrey Show*

Wooden, John: American basketball coach most noted for leading UCLA to ten national championships in twelve years.

Ziglar, Zig: American author and motivational speaker

Sources

- about.com
- africanamericanquotes.org/confidence.html
- *The American Heritage® Dictionary of the English Language, Fourth Edition.*
- americaslibrary.gov
- answers.com
- bbc.co.uk
- biblegateway.com
- brainyquote.com
- Christian-quotes.com
- dictionary.reference.com/browse/inspiration
- dressforsuccess.org
- ellafitzgerald.com
- *Encarta Webster's College Dictionary: 2nd Edition* (2005)
- *Essence.* March 2007, pg 194.
- famousquotesandauthors.com
- goodreads.com/author/show/149829.Mary_Anne_Radmacher
- gps.gov
- great-quotes.com
- holtgws.com

- hyperdictionary.com
- lifewithconfidence.com
- motivatingquotes.com
- my-inspirational-quotes.com
- newworldencyclopedia.org
- npor.org.uk
- quotemonk.com/quotes/faith_quotes.htm
- quotationspage.com
- patrickoverton.com/bio.html
- quoteland.com
- quotes-of-wisdom.eu
- schulersolutions.com/resistance_to_change.html Copyright (c) 2003
- *Sister Act 2: Back in the Habit.* Touchstone Pictures, 1993
- thinkexist.com
- tsowell.com
- Ultraoz.50megs.com
- web.mit.edu
- Wikipedia.com
- wisdomquotes.com
- Youquoted.com

The Empowered Speaker Company

The Empowered Speaker is a company focused on coaching others to become more confident and dynamic public speakers. The company specializes in public speaking workshops leveraging the Speakers Training Camp program.

Speakers Training Camp workshops are customizable in length to meet the needs of corporations, colleges, and organizations. One-on-one coaching is also available for individuals.

Christy Demetrakis is available for seminars on improving public speaking and personal communication skills. Christy is also available as a keynote speaker. For more information on how Christy can help your company or organization or you personally, visit www.empoweredspeaker.com.

Subscribe to www.empoweredspeaker.com/blogs for tips and advice on public speaking and presentation skills.

Contact Christy Demetrakis:
Christy@empoweredspeaker.com